My Path to Praise

A Private Journey from Hell

My Path to Praise

A Private Journey from Hell

Rosalind Gail Smith

Dove
Publishers

My Path to Praise: A Private Journey from Hell
Published by
Dove Christian Publishers
P.O. Box 611
Bladensburg, MD 20710-0611
www.dovechristianpublishers.com

Library of Congress Control Number: 2017962484

ISBN: 978-0-9986690-7-6

Printed in the United States of America

Table of Contents

Dedications vi

Disclaimer ix

Foreword x

Introduction 1

Wide is the Path to Hell 9

The Inward Struggle/Invisible Chains 19

Fear was My Foe 25

My Soul Escaped 35

Miracles Just Happen 41

The Alabaster Box 43

Conclusion 47

Psalm 23 50

The Oak Tree 51

Meditation Scriptures: 52

Final Thought 53

More About The Author: 54

Notes/ Confessions 57

Acknowledgements 59

Dedications

This poem is dedicated to a young man named Mike whom I believe God sent to me. I call him my angel.

He's the image of a spiritual being.
This I can tell just by seeing.
He lifts me up so very high
That I could almost touch the sky.
He's a messenger who brings me hope, who brings me joy,
who brings me love; most of all he understands and
never have I seen such a Godly man.
Sometimes I see something I can't figure out,
what is this man really all about?
Behind every man lies a mystery,
this man is calm and peaceful, just like the sea.
The waves come across so very clear,
but behind that smile lies a healthy fear.
There's a fear of revealing that person unknown
so maybe it's better he's not shown.
I didn't always know just how to respond,
but one thing's for sure we have a great bond.
We met up one morning as I was on my way
to death and destruction, I'm sure he would say.
He explained his purpose, his reason for being there.
It was the spirit inside of him that led him to share.
As he proceeded to explain how his life used to be a
mess,
he looked at me and said take my shoulder and rest.

I began to weep uncontrollably
as I saw my life flash before me.
He promised he would be there no matter what the cost.
I knew then all was not lost.
From that moment on I knew I had a friend
even though I continued deep in my sin.
He gave me his card and said call if you want to talk,
but regretfully as I was, I wasn't ready to take that spiritual walk.
I lied, I cheated, I even used my new friend
but the spirit inside would not let it end
He took me to church, he did all he could.
Right then the yoke was broken, I knew where I stood.
My life got a little better as God became my love.
My heart became light as a feather,
my spirit quiet as a dove.
From then until now my faith gets stronger,
I thank God every day I'm not there any longer.
As for my new friend, he's still there for me
Because like I said before he's everything a Godly man
can be.

To my grandmother, Mamie Hester:

Thank you grandmom for loving me through it all. The last time we were together, I promised I would turn my life around, and I did. I wish you were here to witness my love for Christ. I'm sure you're among the great cloud of witnesses cheering me on. Although I was incarcerated when God called you home, I never doubted your love for me. You gave the best hugs, and I enjoyed our long rides to Dublin, Georgia on that great big Greyhound bus every summer. You made me laugh when you instructed me not to call you grandmom. Instead, you said I should call you mom because no one would believe you were my grandma; you looked so young. And you always smelled so sweet. I'm sorry for the times you witnessed the consequences of my addiction. I miss you, grandmommy, and I love you so much.

After all I have been through, I never felt so separated from her. The chaplain assigned to my unit assured me that my grandmother knew I loved her. His words gave me comfort and assurance. I cried for days, feeling helpless and separated from my family while they attended her funeral. I was so disappointed in myself, constantly wondering how this could have happened, as if it would have been easier for me to handle if I were released. When I cried out to God, I felt the spirit of the Lord rise up in me. I felt God's steadfast love, his forgiveness, and his comfort. Even though she witnessed some of the consequences of my addiction, I wished I could have spent more time with her in those last days of her life. I wish I could've erased her memories of me in that awful condition and replaced them with memories of my youth. I knew it was God's love that compelled the chaplain to visit my unit. His visit was purposeful; he came to see me—just me.

Disclaimer

Henceforth, some statements attributed to others may not be direct quotes. Instead, they are references from various lessons and teachings from pastors and teachers who have influenced my life throughout the years. This is a book of non-fiction which reflects the author's personal recollection of events.

Foreword

From my husband:

God has blessed me to be able to witness my wife, Rosalind, blossom into a wonderful, loving, and caring woman of God. I've watched her press through blood, sweat and tears. Life has been very cloudy at times, but once the smoke cleared, there she was, still standing, waiting for the next battle.

I am so proud of my wife for pressing through the issues of life while allowing God to use her to pen her life story in this book. She's not ashamed to remove the veil and allow you to witness the pains and secrets of her past. Your life will never be the same once you read her story. Generational curses will be broken, hearts will be mended, and hope will be restored. This is not your ordinary book; this could very well be your life.

May God bless you,
Servant Wesley

A Daughter's Love

My mother is, by far, one of the strongest, if not the strongest, woman I know. The struggle she has endured has given her a testimony that provides encouragement and hope for all women. The lessons she has taught me have provided me with tools to set my life on a bright path. Therefore, it is my hope that her faith and diligence in sharing God's love will in turn touch you, providing you with guidance and peace in your own lives.

I am very proud of my mother and want everyone to know it is because of her that I have become the woman I am today. Thank You Mom!

Your loving daughter, Asia

From the heart of a friend:

I always knew Rosalind was destined to have two things in life; riches and greatness. She has been blessed with both; one in the form of God's grace, the other God's almighty mercy. Throughout the many years I have known Rosalind, she has always been a strong and determined woman, willing to work hard to accomplish her goals. As a first time author, Rosalind G. Smith has dedicated years to writing this book and sharing her journey of heartache and redemption with her readers. I am so proud of my friend for sharing her intimate journey of true forgiveness, salvation, and freedom.

As a mother, I have had the divine opportunity to watch her raise two beautiful children; both of which any parent would be proud to call their own. Her marriage is grounded in the Lord, and her husband is a dedicated and hardworking Godly man. She is a great daughter, sister and supporting friend. We met in college over 30 years ago. She wanted to be a lawyer. Perhaps that will be her next journey (I wouldn't be surprised!) She is capable of accomplishing anything her heart desires with God's grace and mercy.

It's never too late for you to remember who you are. You're a Godly woman. The woman God intended you to be; It's not too late to dream big dreams and discover that God loves you in ways you cannot imagine. That's what I think of my friend and the life she has allowed God to create for her and her family. Jeremiah 29:11 says, "For I know the plans I have for you, declares the Lord, plans to prosper you and not to harm you, plans to give you hope and a future."

As a friend, I pray all the best for the future of her book and continued blessings in her path to praise! Congratulations Rosalind!

Tina Adams

Introduction

I want to introduce to you the old me. My actions resulted from hurt, pain and out-of-control emotions. But God's grace is real.

"I will praise thee; for I am fearfully and wonderfully made: marvellous are thy works; and that my soul knoweth right well" (Psalms 139:14, KJV)

It's epic, heroic, monumental and narrative. The drama is real and intense. Yet, God's legendary power of healing and deliverance is real only to remember that the "... *that they overcame him by the blood of the Lamb, and by the word of their testimony; and they loved not their lives unto the death"* (Revelations 12:11, KJV)

Thank you Lord for your grace and mercy upon my life, your mercy does endure forever.

I grew up in a middle-upper-class neighborhood in Philadelphia Pennsylvania. My family consisted of an older brother and younger sister. My mother was and still is a true matriarch. She is the type of woman who demands respect by ruling her home well. She was estranged from my father and later married my first stepfather. Surprisingly enough, that time wasn't so bad because we got along very well. This was largely due to my biological father's regular visits when he wasn't traveling around the world as a Merchant Marine. It was as if I had two dads at the same time. That was great! Later on, at the age of sixteen, I learned of my father's death; he had a heart attack. From that moment, something happened to me. I felt my heart drop after my mother shared the news. I was speechless for several weeks. I couldn't believe it. My father was gone. How could that be? I felt abandoned, and my life began to change. I felt like the wicked witch in the Wizard of Oz just melting down to nothing. I remembered feeling a tremendous loss. As a result, I was constantly depressed, experiencing low self-esteem, never fitting in anywhere or with anyone. I felt like a lonely girl living in a bubble. I sat in that bubble watching the world pass me by. Everyone around me, including some of my high school and middle school friends, seemed to be so happy. They seem to have it all together. They seem to know what they wanted out of life. I wanted something other than my own life. I just didn't know what it was; I didn't know how to achieve it, and I didn't know how to explain it.

My father acted as my shield of protection. When he was around nothing else seems to matter. We had so many happy moments. My happiest moments with my dad was when I went to restaurants with him as his date for the night. We both loved seafood. I was just like my dad. We had picnics in the park, and we had long talks sitting in his canary yellow Cadillac while he told me all about the birds and the bees and the do's and don'ts. I can only remember having two or three close friends, one of whom was my father because I found it difficult to trust anyone, especially other girls in my age group. I just couldn't find trust or integrity among them.

Several years passed before my stepfather died from heart failure; that was another major disenchantment in my life. During my teenage years and early adulthood, my mother and I couldn't seem to get along. I fought with her all the time. That led me from sadness to anger which always ended in confusion. My soul was a cellar full of pain, fear, and anxiety. Every day I watched my friends and their moms hang out together and do special things together. I knew I was missing out on something. But despite all of that, my mom instilled good morals and values in me.

As a result, I managed to put myself through college and acquire several degrees. I was determined to live on campus even though I lived fifteen minutes away from home. It was my great escape! Basically, I needed to get out of my mother's house, live on my own, do my own thing and make my own decisions. I didn't realize that I was trying to find myself. Satan was also seeking whom he could devour and destroy. He got a good head start. Satan made his moves in my life. And since I didn't have God to rely on, I was defenseless and weaponless. I was not prepared for what was to become a suicide mission to hell.

I went through my entire childhood and early adult life not knowing who in the hell I was. I just didn't know my purpose. Why was I born? What was my mission? Where did I belong? What role was I supposed to play? Who were the characters in my life, and what were their roles? I wondered if I could play *my* part right. To me, life was one big show where the characters all had their roles.

However, the role that was handed to me never seemed to fit. You know, being who everyone wanted me to be, saying all the right things, and definitely looking the part, even though I was always told I was too skinny. Compared to the other girls, they were right. So I bought into the lie that I had to have the big legs and big booty to be accepted, especially by the more popular boys. They ignored me anyway. Could it have been because of this awful rash I used to have on the back of my legs, arms, and neck, not to mention my allergies and hay fever that haunted me like a plague? Every conversation was disrupted by three or four sneezes. I hated it! I felt so imperfect, ugly, and sickly. I was a mess. So I thought.

Boys in college were my temporary fixes. It was easy for me to blame my mother for all my miseries, but it wasn't her fault. My mother did the best she could. She was a hard-working woman who made sure her children had the best of everything. Finally, after a victorious battle with lupus, my mom received Jesus Christ into her life. She managed to lead all her children to Christ and has been on fire for God ever since.

Back then I hated my mother because of the death

of my fathers. I even hated that I was born. However, to this day I applaud her endurance and long-suffering. I couldn't figure out how she managed to endure the effect of two dead husbands.

I was an angry person because I had no friends and I was petite. I also hated myself for not having the nerve to continue my education and attend law school. I felt as if I had been cheated. I had strong feelings of bitterness, hatred, and unforgiveness dwelling deep down inside of me. With my entire world spinning out of control, my mother decided to remarry again. That husband later died of cancer. I couldn't figure out what was going on in my life, but I knew for sure I would never marry or allow anyone to get close to me. I did not realize God had other plans for me.

Once I completed college in 1982, I experimented with drugs and alcohol. I thought I had finally filled the void in my life. I started with a little alcohol and marijuana, and then I found myself freebasing cocaine. When I graduated to crack cocaine, I started feeling accepted in affluent circles which otherwise would never give me the time of day, including some famous artists whose names I do not care to mention. Now we had something in common; drinking, drugging and a satanic death wish. For many years, I'd managed to fool everyone. I kept my job and always looked good on the outside, yet was dying and broke on the inside. The deception didn't last long. The man I lived with for ten years found me in the bathroom with an empty bottle of pills next to me. Obviously, my suicide attempt had failed. Getting my stomach pumped was one of the worst feelings in the world. I later woke up in the hospital feeling so disappointed that I'd failed. It wasn't a happy time for me because I had nothing to live for other than depression and misery.

After a few short years, my life started to spiral out of control. I lost everything, and I started to go insane. I'd lost my desire to live, so I attempted suicide a second time. I couldn't seem to do anything right, not even kill myself. I just wouldn't die! I kept waking up to more misery.

By the world's standards, my life consisted of a succession of rehabs and detox centers. I must say that each time I was released, I acquired a little more hope. I really believed I was free from those demons; healed, set free and all better.

I thought I would become a perfect person with a perfect life. Then I met my daughter's father, who made me pregnant only to begin that vicious cycle of drugs again. Now I had a partner in sin. Boy, was I deceived. Not only did we use drugs together, but there was an unborn child at risk. We were recovering addicts, which was an obvious recipe for relapse. We found comfort in each other because we cosigned each other's misery. We deceived ourselves and each other. Our death wish was camouflaged as love. It wasn't love. We were both sick in our addictions! We were confused about life and our purpose for our existence. We loved each other through the eyes of an addict. I believe if we would have met under different circumstances the outcome may have been different. But even through all my disappointments, he is still a wonderful father to our daughter.

Thank God for my mother. We both became born-again Christians while Asia, our daughter, was still in my womb. Psalm 51, a psalm of repentance, was our daily devotion. Although I didn't understand what It all meant, I read it anyway. I believe this is why my daughter is alive and well today at 28. The doctors told me she would be physically deformed with many birth defects. They also said her brain would not function properly. In other words, she would not have a chance at being normal. But the doctors didn't realize that I had a praying mother. Even though I used drugs six out of the nine months of my pregnancy, my mom cared for me in my last trimester. I remember her hands feeling warm on my body as she anointed me with oil every night with prayer. As a result, Asia was born normal. There wasn't a trace of drugs in her body or mine. God's grace and mercy were obvious to everyone except me. Even after that miracle, I returned to drugs, leaving my mom to care for my daughter. I was now jobless and living off welfare, which I eventually used to support my habit. When rehab, NA, and AA didn't work, I tried to relocate, somehow thinking it would all go away. But I found out that wherever I went, there I was.

Now I would like to invite you to explore, journey

and reflect back with me to a life of pain and self-destruction. My life was defined as *"the making of a bomb."*

That's when personalities within oneself conflict with each other. It's a constant warfare. It doesn't take a lot of materials to make a bomb. Just spirits unwilling to submit, surrender, or humble themselves for Christ.

There is ultimate destruction. BOOM!!!!!!!!!!!!!!!!!!!!!!

I challenge you to allow God to defuse that time bomb within you as I have done. Are you subject to your own personal ticking bomb?

"Blessed are they whose iniquities are forgiven, and whose sins are covered. Blessed is the man to whom the Lord will not impute sin" (Romans 4:7-8, KJV).

HIS MERCY ENDURES FOREVER!

Wide is the Path to Hell

"Enter through the narrow gate. For wide is the gate and broad is the road that leads to destruction, and many enter through it. But small is the gate and narrow the road that leads to life, and only a few find it" *(Matthew 7: 13-14, NIV).*

I was so excited to receive my first real job after graduating college. I worked with neglected, deprived and abused teenage girls at a residential facility. Not only did my new friends introduce me to themselves, but they also introduced me to freebasing cocaine, another word for crack. It started out so much fun and thrilling. There was a sense of euphoria in my high that it made me feel so powerful. Initially, we started to get high only on the weekends. Later on, we found every excuse to get high, including holidays, birthdays, anniversaries, New Year's Eve, and any other day we felt like celebrating. Hours turned into days, days turned into months and months turned into years. I finally realized I had developed an addiction. I couldn't do without it. I was no longer productive in my career, and the few friends I had begun to diminish. I became estranged from my family, and my personality changed from being selfless to becoming selfish. My mood swings were so erratic that no one wanted to be around me.

My boyfriend, whom I lived with for ten years, and I began to get high together. The only difference between him and me was that he was able to control himself. He could stop whenever he wanted to, and that made me so angry with him. He tried to warn me that my demise was soon to come, but I didn't believe him. I had become a different person. After many nights of hanging out all night long, missing days of work, and isolating myself, that relationship eventually dissolved. My sense of self-worth dissolved as well. He couldn't help me, Lord knows he tried. My life was a mess. Even in the midst of my psychosis, the Lord continued to take me from danger. There were many instances in which, by all rights, I should be dead. Knives were placed at my throat, guns put to my head, and I was raped several times and left for dead. By His Mercy, I always escaped death. My addiction left me homeless and physically unable to hold any jobs. I and several others lived under a bridge in Florida.

This is where my drug addiction took me.

We had our own little community right off Sistrunk, a main highway in Florida. It was scary at times, but I had no other recourse. So, to survive, I developed a 'sticky fingers' habit. I had to find a way to provide privacy for myself while living under that awful bridge. So, I found several thrift stores to steal from.

The items I stole were very essential to me, essential to my life; therefore, I felt the sin of stealing them was justified. Those items were curtains, which I hung from one tree branch to the other to separate my area from everyone else's, blankets, socks, pants, shirts, and shoes. Only the necessities for survival. I even stole a knife which I kept for protection against undesirables, including a certain police officer who would later arrest me for solicitation. Little did I know he was protecting me from myself; from my pain; from my heart ache. At least while incarcerated I found rest, food, and shelter.

Even though we were homeless and seeking out our next victim to finance our addiction, we looked out for each other. We protected each other. We shared what we had with each other. No one went without food, drink, or drugs. I thought that would be my lifestyle and my destination forever; I thought I would die there. I couldn't see any way out. I hated myself, but they seemed to love me. We had so much in common--- sin! God knows I tried to tame my sin, that monster, that demon, but I was unsuccessful. There were many times when I even thought that Satan was out of my life, but I allowed him back in as soon as one of my unresolved issues resurface. I didn't realize at the time that I was in spiritual warfare. Although I didn't have a relationship with God Almighty, I somehow knew I was dealing with the devil. He is a liar! He gave me false hope in people who were just like me. They were just as lost as I was with no hope of a real life. I was so deceived. Each moment that I stayed in my addiction resulted in horrific consequences.

At this point, I had lost all hope. Fortunately, the Lord would always touch someone's heart and feed me. However, the crack houses I found myself living in had no running water and no electricity. I used candles for light (Now I am the light of the world!!) Even the rats didn't come nigh my dwelling; they seem to just scurry on by. While I was still living in Philadelphia, my mother would pick me up, drive me home, bathe me, feed me then return me to the crack house I called home. I believed I was meant to live this way. I was so blind. I became accustomed to my own stench; it was no longer offensive to me. I patched the holes in the bottoms of my shoes with pieces of my lost and found clothing. I sometimes wore the same clothing for weeks at a time. I hoped no one I knew would see me because I did not want to embarrass my mother. Her knees were probably already worn out from petitioning God for his mercy upon my life. I think there were times when she prayed that God would take me out of my misery. And I didn't blame her.

There were two things I feared the most: dying in my addiction, and my friend Carrie. I believe she had her watchdogs out on a mission to track me down. She was relentless. She just kept showing up in my life at the most inopportune times. And one day she said, "I'm your friend, that's what friends do." But I couldn't receive it because I was focused on my next high, and there wasn't a chance of manipulating her.

She saw right through my schemes, which led her on a search for rehabilitation centers for me. Sometimes her own home became a place of refuge. Now that's a friend. That's mercy!

I'll never forget the night I was walking down the street on a mission from hell about 3 AM in Florida. A group of men and women whom I know to be missionaries jumped out of their car, surrounded me in a circle and begin praying in what they called the Spirit. When they finished, they jumped back in their cars and left. Just like that! They said God sent them on a mission to pray for me. My feet were stuck; it felt like 30 minutes had gone by before I could move. God's prayer warriors were on a mission that night. Mission accomplished!

Once again, God's grace was with me because I was facing five years at Florida State prison for possession of cocaine and soliciting my body for the cause of my addiction. A few moments before my sentence was to be announced, something happened. Judge Fogel decided to place me in a three-month drug program located within the city jail, away from the general population. By the way, Judge Fogel was a Christian. How about that for grace! It was there that I developed my gift for writing. I begin to write all my feelings down on paper. Of course, I was eventually appointed editor of the jail's newspaper. Believe it or not, I began to realize that God had his hand on my life. I didn't really know what it meant, but I knew He was there. Still, after I was released, I continued in my sin. It's true that when God says he will never leave you nor forsake you, He means it. The Lord had his unique ways of drawing me close to him.

There was a man God used to bring me back into the ark of safety. While continuing to live on the streets in Florida, I would make my way down to a little church on the corner every Wednesday and Sunday night. No matter how high I was, I was determined not to miss those nights. I was drawn there because I could hear their praise and worship music miles away. I stood around the corner clapping my hands, praying that God would find it in his heart to give me another chance. I did want to be delivered. I just didn't know how. I didn't know what to do. I didn't know whom to talk to. I was scared and afraid and lonely. I didn't trust anyone anymore.

So, one day, I got up the nerve to sneak in the back of his church when I thought no one was looking. Somehow, they didn't seem to mind that I was looking bad, smelling even worse and definitely singing off-key. Then one day, a very tall, dark man walked up to me near the church and said that God sent him to pray for me. He said he would pray in the Spirit while laying his hands on my shoulders (I kept hearing about this Holy Spirit). The man was very polite, his voice was low, and his demeanor was very friendly. So, we prayed for me right outside the church in broad daylight. I fell to my knees and wept profusely. I wanted so badly to be delivered from that awful, wicked lifestyle, and God used this man to give me shelter in his sister's home with groceries and a warm bed to sleep in. It only lasted a little while because the sin in the world called me back out to play. During that time, I lived two blocks from my future husband and never knew it. We'd never met. I later found out, after we married, he had been going through the same addiction in the same neighborhood. I guess it wasn't time for us to meet. How bizarre is that!

Sin can be very embarrassing when laced with shame and self-loathing. I felt that. Every time I sought out my next victim to manipulate money, I felt myself slipping deeper and deeper into a pattern of shame. People would stare, point fingers, and whisper nasty remarks about me behind my back. But I heard them. They were right. It reminded me of small children calling me names and throwing rocks at me. They called me dirty girl, stupid girl and insane girl. Now I know how the woman in the Bible felt who was caught in adultery (John 8:1–11). They wanted to stone her, make her pay for her sin. But by God's authoritative power, they knew they could not judge her. He extended mercy, although her sin was real.

Likewise, Jesus defended me too. He extended His love and promised grace and mercy on my life despite what I had done, what I was doing, or what I was continuing to do. I was given countless opportunities to repent. He's such a loving God. He knew my future, but I didn't. I asked myself why I should repent. I had nothing to look forward to, but I didn't realize the plan God had for my life. *"For I know the plans I have for you, declares the Lord, plans to prosper you and not harm you, plans to give you hope and a future"* (Jeremiah 29:11, NIV).

His plan was set from the very beginning. The Bible says he knows every hair on my head. God says, "… He would never leave thee nor forsake thee" (*Hebrews 13:5, KJV),* and He never did.

I know this now, but back then, I was not reassured about anything, especially not my life or God's love. I have become a master of manipulation while playing the blame game. I blamed everyone for the choices I'd made. I often convinced myself if my mom didn't yell so much, I would be okay. If my live-in boyfriend would have been more patient…if I had more friends to talk to…if my fathers had lived a little longer…if I had a better job…if I had gone to law school…if I wasn't so skinny…if my siblings and I had developed a closer brother and sister relationship…If my mother and I hadn't fought so much. If this, if that, if, if, if…

The only thing about the 'blame game' is that no one was there to play with me. As usual, I was alone even in that deceptive theory; all alone at my own pity party.

Well, maybe not all alone, because Satan was there planting seeds of destruction and deception. He was the only unwanted quest who kept showing up, un- invited, pushing his way into my heart.

I was so confused and lonely. Even attending those NA and AA meetings didn't help. They only confused me more because of the typical traditional acknowledgment of addiction. They described my obvious short-lived surrender as a 'HALT,' meaning hungry, angry, lonely, and tired. That was the best description I've heard about myself in a long time. While we were called in the "rooms," we sat around in a circle of sharing our pain with one another, which, I guess, was a type of confession. What I couldn't grasp was the confession. I would say "HI, my name is Rosalind and I'm an addict." But if the Bible says, "*Therefore, if anyone is in Christ, the new creation has come: the old has gone, the new is here*" *(2 Corinthians 5:17, NIV),* then why was I confessing that I was an addict? Something wasn't right. However, at least I had an excuse to justify why I would return to sin. They would understand. After all, I was an addict, right? Or was I? Their entire focus and purpose were to convince me not to pick up another drug. They said, "just don't pick up." Do anything else, 'just don't pick up'; another deceptive lie from Satan. So, I guess sex, manipulation, lying, cheating, stealing was all good. "Just don't pick up"!

HIS MERCY ENDURES FOREVER!

The Inward Struggle/
Invisible Chains

"We know that the law is spiritual; but I am unspiritual, sold as a slave to sin. I do not understand what I do. For what I want to do I do not do, but what I hate I do. And if I do what I do not want to do, I agree that the law is good. As it is, it is no longer I myself who do it, but it is sin living in me. For I know that good itself does not dwell in me, that is, in my sinful nature. For I have the desire to do what is good, but I cannot carry it out. For I do not do the good I want to do, but the evil I do not want to do — this I keep on doing. Now if I do what I do not want to do, it is no longer I who do it, but it is sin living in me that does it" (Romans 7:14-20, NIV).*

I recall my husband preaching a message entitled, "Delivered but Not Yet Free." At first, I didn't understand the spiritual concept, but after many nights of meditation, I received an astounding revelation from the Lord. I was delivered through his word, but I was still bound in my mind by those haunting thoughts of the past. They were my invisible chains. That is, the thoughts that used to plague my mind, will, and emotions were still very much alive, and I couldn't figure out why these thoughts continued to haunt me. I was set free from the memories of drug abuse, prostitution, hurts and pains and the pain I caused to others. I wasn't free from the pain and heartache of being lonely. I wasn't free from the memories of all the fights my mother and I used to have; I wasn't free of wondering if I could ever have any real friends. I wasn't free from the torment of not knowing if I will ever be used by God; if I would ever make a difference in this lost and dying world. I wasn't free from those things because I didn't allow my deliverance to manifest itself in my life because I was faithless. The Bible talks about having the faith the size of a mustard seed. But even that mustard seed of faith seemed to be so huge, so big and so unattainable.

So instead of embracing my deliverance, I allowed the past thoughts to interrogate my life; where I found myself bound again by Satan's tactics. There were many times I found myself repeating the same mistakes; returning to those same people, places, and things.

Repeating old habits are inevitable when we don't understand why we do what we do and where it comes from. I can't stress enough how important it is to identify the demons assigned by Satan. Some of our issues result from generational sin.

Unknowingly, we reap some of the same habits and behaviors of our ancestors such as our mothers, fathers, and grandparents. We perish for lack of knowledge, Knowledge is power! It's important to know why we do what we do, and we must learn how to denounce generational sins. If not, we'll live our lives infecting others with our misery and sinful behaviors.

The devil's job is to torment us. To make us feel bad about ourselves. He makes us feel useless, lost, and afraid to prosper and succeed. He makes us feel unlovable with the inability to love ourselves or others. The bible says that we are fearfully and wonderfully made *(Psalms 139:14).*

God says we are the head, not the tail *(Deuteronomy 28:13).* God has his way of making us feel so very special.

"What, then, shall we say to these things? If God is for us, who can be against us? He who did not spare his own son, but gave him up for us all – how will he not also, along with him, graciously give us all things? ...No, in all these things we are more than conquerors through him who loved us." (Romans 8:31-32;37, NIV).

God loves us when no one else cares; when everyone else leaves and when all seems hopeless. He's just that kind of God. He loves us when we don't love ourselves. There were so many invisible intimidating tactics of the enemy that seemed so real and so true. But God reminds us that the tactics of the enemy are mere shadows of death designed to snatch away any chance of deliverance. The devil is evil!

The late Whitney Houston sang a song entitled, "I Wanna Dance with Somebody (Who Loves Me)." You may ask why I identified with this song. There is a verse in that song which says, "when the night falls, my lonely heart calls…I wanna dance with some-body." So, when I say I was delivered but not yet free, it's because of the many times I'd asked God to save me. And HE did! But my soul was a cellar full of pain, fear, and anxiety and my mind was gripped with the fear of not becoming the woman God intended for me. My heart was still broken in so many places it seemed impossible to fix. My past hurts and pains seemed to take residence in my present life. Because I didn't know what God expected of me, I did what was familiar to me. When nighttime would come, my heart became lonelier. It was something about night-time, it's when I decided to dance with the devil, a two-step waltz to hell. He was my private dancer. It was a private journey to hell.

But despite my lonely thoughts and rendezvous with Satan, I realize that God was watching over me, especially at night:

"He will not let your foot slip—he who watches over you will not slumber; indeed, he who watches over Israel will neither slumber nor sleep. The Lord watches over you – the Lord is your shade at your right hand; the sun will not harm you by day, nor the moon by night. The Lord will keep you from all harm – he will watch over your life. The Lord will watch over your coming and going both now and forevermore" (Psalms 121:3-8, NIV).

There were many times when I felt so lonely in this great big world, constantly asking myself where I fit in and what was I born to do, what was my purpose. When I asked myself those questions, I didn't have a relationship with God. I didn't even know him as a personal savior. In my addiction, I felt like giving up so often, unless I knew someone cared. But for the most part, I didn't think anyone loved me or cared that I existed. I didn't fit any standards or anyone's idea of a person. I considered myself the invisible, lost girl.

There is always a warfare, battle, and struggle that goes on inside of us, but I didn't know how to fight spiritually. Depression got the best of me. Depression is real. It's a dark place the devil has reserved for people with unresolved issues. He tries to make us believe that our primary residence is on a street called 'depression.' Depression isolates, it hurts, it's painful and creates a lonely vacuum. And if you're not careful, others can be sucked into the madness of your low self-esteem. I can talk about it now because I see it for what it is. It's a deception, a false sense of being. I remember my depression becoming a constant drip, annoying and irritating me. Every time I thought I was fixed, it showed up again.

Thank God for teachings by Pastor Jones. I've learned to deal with the source, not the symptoms. My remedy is God my Savior. My hope is in Jesus Christ because there is hope beyond our situations. My life is based on my redemption through Jesus Christ. I'm finally able to see the light into my future, as I was a woman marked by God from the beginning. *"And we know in all things God works for the good of those who love him, who have been called according to his purpose" (Romans 8:28, NIV).*

HIS MERCY ENDURES FOREVER!

Fear was My Foe

The Lord is my light and my salvation — whom shall I fear? The Lord is the stronghold of my life — of whom shall I be afraid?

(Psalm 27:1, NIV)

My life was on autopilot; nonstop insanity was what I'd become used to, afraid to really feel anything. I was void of emotions, and I was afraid of *me*. I just couldn't shake the feeling that I would never accomplish *anything*. I didn't know God during those challenging times in my life. Therefore, I didn't know how to face my fears. My fears were masked with fake smiles and fake friends, and I was afraid of my own insecurities. If someone said they didn't like me, in my mind, it was my fault. If I had failed at something, it was my fault. If something didn't go quite right, then something must have been wrong with me. One of my biggest challenges was feeling that I was not good enough to attend law school. Despite my constant and consistent honors and high grades, I just didn't think I was good enough.

I was afraid my father would leave me, and he eventually died when I was sixteen. I was afraid I would grow up with no friends, and I did. I was afraid I would never have strong relationships with my siblings, and I didn't. I was afraid I would die lonely, and I *did* (I eventually died to myself and became alive in Christ). I was afraid that if I had children, we would always fight and argue just like my mother and I. I was scared to death of generational curses. Thank God the snare is now broken and I have escaped the plagues, hardships, and disappointments of generational scars.

Fear had a hold on my mind, my body, my emotions, and my life decisions. My life was affected by the very word itself, *fear.*

Even though I operated in generational sins, my scars have healed through the power of Christ and his amazing love.

Generational curses are not only real but astonishingly true. For instance, I never really knew my uncle, my mother's brother. My son has not known his uncle, my brother. And my daughter has not yet had a consistent relationship with her brother because of geographical locations. Just the thought of my daughter growing up without her brother frightens me. The worst fear is of the unknown and the "what ifs."

The fear of raising a child was so real that I tried hard to abort my daughter. I was afraid that if I carried and delivered my daughter full-term, she would grow up to hate me for getting high while carrying her in my womb. So, one night I was at home feeling all alone and sorry for myself. I made a conscious decision to abort her by my own hands. I climbed in the bathtub with a long, outstretched wire hanger. With tears in my eyes, I inserted that hanger in my womb through my vagina. Crying and scared, blood started to stream out of me. I thought I did it! I remember thinking I might kill two birds with one stone. Maybe I could die at the same time, and we would go to heaven together. I sat there in the bloody water and fell asleep, a deep sleep.

I woke up to birds chirping outside my window and the sun shining brightly as it had always done in the morning. The birds were chirping loudly, much like what you would hear in the park during an early-morning walk, I thought they were trying to wake me up. I had been asleep for hours. After waking up, I tried hard to focus because my eyes were so swollen from crying myself to sleep. I looked down in the bathtub, and there was NO BLOOD! That's right, you heard me. NO BLOOD! I was astonished and confused. Until this day I don't know if I dreamed the entire situation or God had saved me from myself again. The hanger was still laying in the bathtub next to me. What's your conclusion?

When God has a plan for your life, we can do nothing to stop it. When he opens a door, no one can close it. When he said ask, believe, and it will be given, he means that. When he says seek and ye shall find, knock, and the door shall be opened, he means that. I say this because the entire day before I tried to abort my daughter, I had read Psalm 51 over, and over, and over again.

"Have mercy on me, God,
according to your unfailing love;
according to your great compassion blot out my trans-
gressions.
Wash away all my iniquity
and cleanse me from my sin.
For I know my transgressions,
and my sin is always before me.
Against you, you only, have I sinned
and done what is evil in your sight;
so you are right in your verdict
and justified when you judge.
Surely I was sinful at birth,
sinful from the time my mother conceived me.
Yet you desired faithfulness even in the womb;
you taught me wisdom in that secret place.
Cleanse me with hyssop, and I will be clean;
wash me, and I will be whiter than snow.
Let me hear joy and gladness;
let the bones you have crushed rejoice.
Hide your face from my sins
and blot out all my iniquity.
Create in me a pure heart, O God,
and renew a steadfast spirit within me.
Do not cast me from your presence
or take your Holy Spirit from me.
Restore to me the joy of your salvation
and grant me a willing spirit, to sustain me.

Then I will teach transgressors your ways,
so that sinners will turn back to you.
Deliver me from the guilt of bloodshed, O God,
you who are God my Savior,
and my tongue will sing of your righteousness.
Open my lips, Lord,
and my mouth will declare your praise.
You do not delight in sacrifice, or I would bring it;
you do not take pleasure in burnt offerings.
My sacrifice, O God, is a broken spirit;
a broken and contrite heart
you, God, will not despise.
(Psalm 51, NIV).

David, the author of this Psalm, was so sorry for what he had done to Bathsheba's husband, and I was sorry too; But I didn't know how to help myself. God only knows that I did not want to expose an innocent child to my madness. But God still had a plan. He didn't abort his plan for my life the way I tried to abort my child.

Later that day my mom came to my apartment to take me to a rehabilitation center. She snapped a Polaroid picture of me while in that awful state of depression (see below). I was wearing red pajamas, and my hair was all over my head. She held me so tight and whispered in my ear that Jesus loved me, and he would never leave me nor forsake me. She then made me promise not to ever get rid of that picture. She said it would always be a testimony of God's goodness. She said I would look back one day to give Him praise. And she was right!

I'd hurt her and so many others that I was willing to do anything to make up for my horrible behavior. There were so many days when she tried to rescue

(Isa. 59:1)
MAY '89

Photo of the author in May 1989

me; so many failed attempts. But this time was different. I knew God was real. After the bathtub incident, I remember thinking, there must be a God and that the holy spirit my mother kept talking about must be real. So, I decided to give God a try. God knows I had nothing else to lose.

Fear was so apparent in my life that I held onto unhealthy relationships, namely my drug-dealing boyfriend. I met him on a celebration cruise yacht, right after I graduated college. He was so handsome with that 'Philadelphia swag.' When I asked what he did for a living, he confessed that he was a drug dealer. It didn't even phase me. Honestly, I thought it was exciting. I thought I was doing something no one else did; I thought I had a prize. I remember staring out of my living room window waiting for him to pick me up for our next date. He swept me off my feet! I had a lot of free time because I hadn't gotten a job yet after graduating. So, I was available to hang out with him every day and all day.

I didn't care that my life was in danger. I didn't care that we could get arrested, and I didn't care what people thought. I thought he was amazing, and I wasn't afraid to let him know. I was his woman, and he was my man. Nothing else mattered because I felt I was on top of the world. We shopped in the most expensive stores, and we dined every day in the high-end restaurants where the elite hung out. I didn't care that my life was in danger as we delivered drugs to doctors, lawyers, famous singers and others. He used me to hold his drugs as we traveled throughout the city of Philadelphia. We made more deliveries than the UPS during a day. I didn't realize that by holding his drugs, I could be arrested for possession and intent to sell. I would be the one to go to jail. But thank God that never happened. Just another merciful escape through God's grace! I was so stupid I didn't even care.

But, when he would leave me in the car for a few minutes I would steal his cocaine from his packages. He had so much that he never even missed it. The cocaine I stole was later used to share with my friend Tina to pump us up for our next job interview. It seemed to make us feel bolder. One of our job interviews required that we travel on the bus from Philadelphia to Virginia. We were interviewing to be airline stewardesses. Can you imagine an airline stewardess high on cocaine while serving passengers alcohol and pretzels? What a joke! But needless to say, we never got the job. Could it be because we were high as a kite?

Anyway, I admired Mel because everyone looked up to him. They bowed down to him. He was so important. We rode in the best cars, shopped until we dropped for days, and it was fun. He held my hand and wasn't afraid to show his affection. I felt so alive. The joy was not because of the things we had. It was because I knew he saw me; he recognized me; he gave me validated attention, especially on dinner dates the way my father used to before he died at 55 years old. He validated my very existence. He reminded me of my dad. He was neat, clean, well put together and a real ladies man just like my dad. And I admired that. I was happy.

I realize now I just wanted the world to know I was alive! Mel knew I was alive! However, all good things must come to an end. After I became employed, we continued to date, but things weren't the same. So, I broke it off with him because I got tired of being "the other woman." Yep, he was married with children. I was so afraid of life that I expected the worst and compromised my integrity just for a lot of attention. It would be several years before I became officially addicted to drugs. I was, without question, addicted to him. My dad was the only man who had given me that kind of attention.

HIS MERCY ENDURES FOREVER!

My Soul Escaped

*"We have escaped like a bird from the fowler's snare; the snare has **been** broken; and we have escaped. Our help is in the name of the Lord, the Maker of heaven and earth."*

(Psalm 124:7-8, NIV)

Somewhere along the line in the midst of my insanity, someone told me about a Christian program called Mission Teens, located in New Jersey. Their only requirement was for me to have a desire to change my life through the power of God. I immediately qualified. As I progressed, I was transferred to several of their locations in three different states. It was there that I finally had a made-up mind to serve God no matter what the cost.

I met a man named Rob. He was the director of the Mission Teens. He was tall and absolute about his purpose in life. His smile was wide, and his voice was deep. His face was friendly enough for me to trust him. Later that evening on my first day he found me sitting in the middle of the floor in the room to which I was assigned. My emotions were mixed with fear of a new environment and gratitude that God rescued me from myself and that horrific lifestyle of drug abuse.

While feeling sorry for myself, Rob introduced me to an amazing scripture in the Bible. *"Therefore, since we have been justified through faith, we have peace with God through our Lord Jesus Christ, through whom we have gained access by faith into his grace in which we now stand. And we boast in the hope of the glory of God. Not only so, but we also glory in our sufferings, because we know that suffering produces perseverance; perseverance, character; and character, hope. And hope does not put us to shame, because God's love has been poured out into our hearts through the Holy Spirit, who has been given to us"* (Romans 5:1-5, NIV)

I know now that my suffering was not in vain. I was created for greatness, prosperity, and significance. Suffering is a character builder; without pain, there would be no gain. But even so, I was still blinded by so much hurt as a child; so much neglect; I had lived in confinement in my own mind. I knew God rescued me. Slowly I liked myself a little more every day. It was okay to look in the mirror again. Smiles turned into laughter and laughter into joy. My favorite time was morning and evening devotions. I developed a strong passion for worship because I love to sing, clap my hands, and stomp my feet. I felt God move on the inside of me. I felt his love and comfort. Lord knows I cried a lot of tears there. One day was particularly joyous for me when I noticed a sign on the wall which read, *"What appeared to be the end is really only a new beginning."* Wow! For the first time, I was assured that I could start over again.

After completing the required eight months, I was given the opportunity to remain as a counselor at another location in Fort Lauderdale, Florida. I accepted the offer with the condition that I could bring my daughter to live with me; she was just beginning to walk. It was great at first until my flesh became restless. I eventually walked out of that mission because I couldn't have my way. I didn't want to be told what to do or where I could go. As time passed, my affection was directed at another resident, which was against their rules. So instead of allowing them to transfer me to another facility, my pride got the best of me, and I walked out. Just like that! My mom arrived there from Philadelphia to take my daughter back home with her. After that, I lived on the streets, in crack houses, and under a bridge for close to a year and was incarcerated in the Broward County Jail. I was delivered, but not yet free. I didn't know how to walk in my deliverance, so I found myself catering to my emotions. Pastor Jones often says that Satan fights God in our minds. And when we give into his tactics, it's a sure sign that our minds are not renewed.

I carried a strong spirit of rejection; it followed me like a plague. It controlled my decisions in every thought I allowed myself to think. It made me afraid to trust anyone, especially women. I hated to hear the word 'no' because that meant you didn't like me. It meant I wasn't good enough. Now I realize that I sabotaged any healthy relationships because of the hurt and pain from my childhood. I viewed everything through a negative filter because I didn't know how to think. I pushed people away, and I wanted no one to get close because I would anticipate a short-lived relationship. Therefore, I lived alone with my thoughts of worthlessness.

I wondered if my brother and sister would ever become my friends. I thought I would have a better chance with them than with someone I didn't know. I grew up so disappointed because they didn't seem to notice me either. I grew up with the brother who loved women and a sister who loved her freedom so much she'd never allow anything or anyone to hold her back — a true renegade, fun-loving and free-spirited. When we became of age, we all went our separate ways, living our own lives and doing our own thing. But deep down inside, I knew they loved me because I sure loved them.

If my memory serves me correctly, once my brother tried to rescue me from my mother. My mom and I had a fight in the basement. She was determined to smack the *you-know-what* out of me because, as usual, I said something I should not have. So, I'm sure I deserved anything I had coming to me. I was always running my mouth, saying things I shouldn't have said; *smelling myself,* as our elders say; trying to be grown. She locked the door so that no one could come downstairs. My brother ran out of the front door and around to the back door in a matter of two minutes. He was determined to intervene; anything to keep my mom from hitting me. He succeeded! When I realized he rescued me, I knew he was my friend and not just my brother.

I previously mentioned residing in several locations of Mission Teens. Well, my final transfer was to Michigan. The temperature there was 45 below zero. They called us the frozen chosen. It was there that I met my soon-to-be husband, Wesley. The Lord began to use us to start a Bible class every evening after our devotions. Under the inspiration of the Holy Spirit, we would encourage everyone to come out of his or her room and join us. Eventually, there were 10 to 15 residents in attendance. It was there that I learned how to pray, to intercede, and to wage war against the enemy. God revealed my gift of intercession. I had developed into a true prayer warrior. I developed a strong sense of discernment, which I now recognize as a gift from God. With regard to Wesley, I can honestly say that the Lord really blinded my eyes because I never really saw his outer man. I found myself attracted to his godliness. He was always so high-spirited and unrestrained. He continually allowed the character of God to overflow his being. I had known no one with such a hunger and desire to serve the Lord. He was the type of man you just wanted to be around because his motives and desires were pure. Through Wesley, I learned it was okay to cry. I wanted to be broken, and let it all out, the way he did. That is what I was attracted to!

Every day was a new day, a day I anticipated seeing him. The more I saw him broken, the brighter I saw him shine. Finally, we left Michigan together. I went home to Philadelphia, and Wesley lived in Maryland with his sister and her family. His family has been a blessing to us. I have the best in-laws on this side of heaven.

Wesley and I never dated but married three months after we left Michigan. We were wed on June 11, 1994, at Rhema Christian Center in Washington, D.C. with Bishop Clarence Givens as our pastor. One of the members, Denise, whom I consider a very close friend to this day, offered me the use of her wedding gown and she didn't even know me at the time.

I am grateful to say, my soul escaped.

HIS MERCY ENDURES FOREVER!

Miracles Just Happen

Besides saying 'yes' to Jesus, I believe my children are my greatest accomplishment. My daughter, Asia, was subject to so much abuse while in my womb.

I used drugs six of the nine months I carried her. I was convinced that it didn't matter because I'd already decided to have an abortion. But while in my addiction I'd lost track of time. The days went by quickly and the months, even quicker. Before I knew it, it was too late to have an abortion. God had other plans. His word says that *"As the heavens are higher than the earth, so are my ways higher than your ways and my thoughts than your thoughts"* (Isaiah 55:9, NIV)

I needed help!!!! That's when my mom stepped in. During my last trimester, she cared for me 24 hours a day. She fed me, bathed me, and anointed me with oil every night. My brother's old bedroom was converted into a place of healing, a refuge, and a spiritual hospital. She was my very own private nurse—nurse Cynthia. We were happy to know that Asia was born healthy. There was no trace of drugs in her body or mine. What a miracle!! We counted all 10 fingers and 10 toes; they were all there. We were amazed that her first hospital picture depicted a pose with Asia using her finger to indicate an 'O.K.' sign. I cried when I saw that; she was actually telling me that everything would be okay, including our lives together as mother and daughter. It was truly a Kodak moment!

I'm so proud of her; actually, we all are. She's a determined and dedicated young lady. And she's a blessing to all who encounter her. This was one time where I wish I could do it all over again. I lived many years with guilt, wondering what she would think once I explained my past life. I've been very transparent with her as much as God would allow. When she experiences struggles, I remind her that God had a plan for her life. Otherwise, she would not have survived my addiction while in my womb. There were times, while in my womb, she would constantly kick me. I often prayed that she would stop! I know now that God used her to stop me in my tracks. She wanted to live! And she did!

Now, she's a 28-year-old college graduate. She's smart and intelligent. She has persevered and endured so many oppositions, so many storms, and so many disappointments. But, despite all of that, she's on her way to a fruitful and prosperous life. God had his hands on her the entire time. She's so beautiful inside and out. She forgives, she loves, and she is loved according to the divine purpose of God!

HIS MERCY ENDURES FOREVER!

The Alabaster Box

"A woman in that town who lived a sinful life learned that Jesus was eating at the Pharisee's house, so she came there with the alabaster jar of perfume. As she stood behind him at his feet weeping, she began to wet his feet with her tears. Then she wiped them with her hair, kissed them and poured perfume on them" (Luke 7:37-38, NIV)

Alabaster was a stone commonly found in Israel. It was a soft stone resembling white marble and is referred to as one of the precious stones used in the decoration of Solomon's Temple (1 Chronicles 29:2, NASB).

Therefore, oil or perfume which was kept in an alabaster jar, vial or vase was preserved until opened. When Mary opened her alabaster box, *"the house was filled with the fragrance of the perfume"* (John 12:3, NIV)

Likewise, God has contained me, preserved me, and kept me until an appointed time. Now that I have been freed and released from the things that had me bound, my aroma is that of my sweet Savior Jesus Christ. There is such a spirit of gratefulness that rests upon my life, my mind, my head, and upon my shoulders. There is a debt I owe and one I could never repay.

I was reluctant to see doctors and therapists because of the stigma attached to those who needed help. I prayed and asked God to please bless me with someone compassionate with the love of Christ in their heart. Because many times I thought no one understood, I would become just another patient, another number and another open file. I've had many therapists who attempted to help me walk through my life to identify the root cause of my issues, especially depression. There was Dr. Lily, who was very committed. She was a Christian woman who prayed with me before and after each session. I believe she was God sent. Then I met Mr. Lawrence at a facility here in Florida. And oddly enough, his last name was Devine. I'm not kidding. Wow! What more could I ask for?

I actually looked forward to our sessions every other week. I knew immediately that he would be more than my therapist. He would also be a lifelong friend of my family as well. When he left that facility, he graciously offered to become my life coach. Who does that? A true man of God who saw a need. What would Jesus do? That's what he would have done. Because Jesus was in control anyway; He set the whole thing up. Oh, and he did house calls, too.

During one session, with my husband present, he suggested an exercise. He said "close your eyes and think of an accident or situation that hurt you the most. Now think about how you would have to reverse that situation."

I thought of the time my mom threw my bird out of the house behind me when I stormed out angrily after an argument with her. My bird sat on the telephone wire above my house for many days. I could do nothing to rescue my bird. I carried that anger for years. I was bitter towards my mother, and that bitterness later turned into resentment. But after reversing the situation in my mind as he suggested, I rescued my bird and live happily ever after, much like a fairy tale. Right then my anger had dissolved and disappeared. Now, when I see or speak with my mom, I never think of that incident at all. Why? Because you can smell the sweet aroma from my alabaster box!

Hallelujah moment

God did an awesome thing when he delivered me from myself. But he did an exceptional thing when he delivered me from being bound and governed by the opinions of others! I'm free now; free to praise him; and I'm free to serve my true and living God, Jesus Christ.

Conclusion

"The Lord is near to all who call on him, to all who call on him in truth. He fulfills the desires of those who fear him; he hears their cry and saves them" (Psalm 145:18-19, NIV).

Generational issues are a virus that will attack every organ in our body. And because it's generational, we find others in our family who carried that same virus or gene. For example, women must get routine breast exams every year. The first question they ask: is there anyone in your family who has had breast cancer? If the answer is yes, then you are now considered at high risk of getting cancer. Now you are instructed to get tested more often than the one who has no cancer in their family. The key is this: if your cancer is detected early enough, it can be usually removed by having one or both breasts removed. If it's not detected early enough, you can certainly die of breast cancer.

God wants us to seek Him in every area of our lives. I pray more often for my family because I have realized that a lot of my issues were generational. As much as my mom and I fought through many hurtful words, I had to revisit the crime scene. I've gone back to Philadelphia to visit with her by divine appointment. I could see so clearly why I did the things I did, why I'd hurt others in the past and why I was so bitter. I'm not saying it was her fault, but I recognized the familiar virus which ran through my family like a thread with no end, strangling me every time someone or something pulled too hard on that thread.

In the Bible, God speaks about Joseph and his many detours on his way to greatness. It was a long journey for Joseph, but those detours and distractions were necessary for Joseph to reach his destiny. Joseph embraced the opportunity God gave him not only to forgive but to bless those who sought to destroy him. I've learned not to harbor bitterness and hatred in my heart anymore and because no one can short-change God's purpose and plan. So, I've forgiven all who have inflicted hurt, harm, and pain upon my life. Because what the devil meant for evil, God turned it into something good. "You intended to harm me, but God intended it for good to accomplish what is now being done, the saving of many lives" *(Genesis 50:20, NIV)*

Even now when trials and detours arise, I sing the lyrics to the song, "Jesus He will Fix It (after awhile)" by Lee Williams and the Spiritual QCs.

When our trunk is finally opened, everything tends to rush out at once; odor after odor; situation after situation; hurt after hurt; pain after pain. It's all there waiting to be released. Your trunk must be opened. Otherwise, the odor remains, and everyone around you will be affected by the stench. Since my past hurts and pains have been healed and revealed, I now smell like my sweet-smelling savior, and I've evolved into a beautiful butterfly! God gave me my wings back, and I intend to fly and soar like an eagle.

My weaknesses have not been a curse because the Lord told Paul that his grace was sufficient. "And he said unto me, My grace is sufficient for thee: for my strength is made perfect in weakness. Most gladly therefore will I rather glory in my infirmities, that the power of Christ may rest upon me" (2 Corinthians 12:9, KJV)

God's grace was sufficient for me all the time....

Psalm 23

The Lord is my shepherd
(That's relationship)
I shall not want   (That's supply)
He maketh me to lie down in green
pastures   (That's rest)
He leadeth me beside still waters   (That's refreshment)
He restoreth my soul (That's healing)
He leadeth me in the path of righteousness (That's guidance)
For His name's sake   (That's purpose)
Yea, though I walk through the valley of the shadow of death
(That's testing)
I will fear no evil   (That's protection)
For thou art with me   (That's faithfulness)
Thy rod and thy staff they comfort me   (That's discipline)
Thou preparest a table before me in the presence of mine enemies
(That's hope)
Thou anointest my head with oil   (That's consecration)
My cup runneth over (That's abundance)
Surely goodness and mercy shall follow me all the days of my life
(That's blessing)
And I will dwell in the house of the Lord   (That's security)
Forever   (That's eternity)

The Oak Tree

Oak trees develop very deep rooting systems that branch off of its main taproot. Over time, the taproot's prominence recedes and is replaced by numerous large lateral roots that form the lateral root system. These lateral roots penetrate the soil 4 feet deep and extend laterally to 90 feet. This is the main part of the root system that supports the tree.[1]

Jesus is our taproot, the strongest part of our foundation, which can't be moved or destroyed. It's the strongest part of us.

So those of you struggling with any addictions, please understand there is hope in Jesus Christ! Jesus loves you, and you are more than what you see in the mirror. You are more than what you've experienced.

You are an overcomer!

You are victorious!

And you are loved!

---

1   Manal, Naima, "The Root System of Oak Trees," *Garden Guides*, September 21, 2017, GardenGuides.com.

Meditation Scriptures:

Romans 7: 4-12 (why)
Matthew 6: 25-34 (seek)
2 Corinthians 6: 14-18 (separate)
James 4: 7-8 (submit)
Ephesians 6: 11 (claim spiritual authority)
Romans 12: 1-2 (transformed mind)
Romans 6: 6-7 (no need to sin)
2 Corinthians 5:17 (new creation)
Psalms 129: 14 (fearfully made)
Jeremiah 29: 11 (His plan)
Jeremiah 1:5 (He knew me)
Romans 8: 31 (more than a conqueror)
Romans 8: 26-30 (my help comes from God)

Final Thought

"For all have sinned and fallen short of the glory of God. And all are justified freely by His grace through the redemption that came by Christ Jesus" (Romans 3: 23-24, NIV)

More About The Author:

God has blessed me with a wonderful family. And He's continuing to restore my relationships one by one. Even though some of the healing in my family is not yet apparent, I am still trusting God for the manifestations thereof. He has given my daughter back whom I once abandoned while in sin. He has blessed me with a wonderful husband, and he has blessed us with a son of miraculous promise. So, I have two miracle children. Only God could do that! So much of my life, while living on the street and being of the world, involved my constantly having to defend myself and looking over my shoulder. Well, as God would have it, He is now my defense, and He commands his angels to watch over me. Now I walk in victory. I believe I am more than a conqueror; I believe God called me out of darkness into his marvelous light, and I believe that God saved me to be the light of the world. **Now that's something to shout about!**

My husband and I work tirelessly side-by-side as we fulfill God's vision to unite churches for the totality of man. God revealed that His miracle will take place through His Ministry, "I Am My Brother's Keeper," a non-profit organization designed to serve the downtrodden and the *whosoever will* (Luke 9:23). Over the years we've overcome many obstacles and come through trials and tribulations. But like Paul the Apostle, we've been able to count them all joy. We've learned to keep the lines of communication open and to put God first in all that we do.

One of our biggest challenges was to give birth to our youngest son Manasseh. All our doctors were totally against our decision because of our history of losing two other children who are now in heaven with Jesus. They told us that he did not have a brain and all his organs would fail. The ultrasounds were their proof. But God was our proof!! Wesley and I decided, with the support of our pastors, to trust God. We fasted and prayed throughout my pregnancy. We truly believed if we could hold fast our confession, that it would be a great recompense of reward. God is true to his word because Manasseh came into this world with the peace of God all over him. He was the happiest baby I'd ever seen and carrying him made me just as happy. We have since dedicated him back to God and vowed to raise him in a godly home. He is our Omega!

And remember those fights I mentioned between my mother and myself, well they have been cast into the sea of forgetfulness, and she has become one of my greatest cheerleaders. What an awesome God we serve!

My husband is my best friend. We have cried together; laughed together; shared together; prayed together, and we are even beginning to look alike. We agree that the church is a wonderful teaching place, but our hearts are in the streets with the lost souls; with the prison-bound; with the homeless; with the prostitutes; with our youth; and with all who will receive Jesus Christ as their personal Lord and Savior! At this point, our faith can move mountains.

One of my many desires is for women to bind together in the unity of love. I believe it is absolutely necessary for women such as myself to be able to support one another and to encourage and pray for one another. We should be able to pray together with the bonds of peace and the *phileo* cords of love binding us together. Once we receive that revelation, there is nothing we can't conquer!

"...Being confident of this, that He who began a good work in you will carry it on to completion until the day of Christ Jesus" (Philippians 1:6, NIV)

HIS MERCY ENDURES FOREVER!

Notes/ Confessions

My prayer for you is that God's demonstration of love and forgiveness has touched your hearts.

List your confessions of sins and issues. Present them to God. He loves you, and He's waiting to hear from you because HIS MERCY ENDURES FOREVER!

"Now unto Him that is able to keep you from falling, and to present you faultless before the presence of His glory with exceeding joy" (Jude 24, KJV).

NOTES_____

_____

_____

CONFESSIONS_____

_____

_____

_____

_____

For More Information

For book order requests, speaking engagements, or workshops, please direct your inquiries to:
P.O. Box 1202
Deerfield Beach, Florida 33441
Phone: (954) 621-6960
Fax: (954) 418-0216
E-mail: rgsmith3@comcast.net
Facebook: Path To Praise

Please visit our website: www.iambkm.org

Acknowledgements

Blessed are the peacemakers: for they shall be called the children of God (Matthew 5:9, KJV)

Thanks to all my co-laborers in Christ for your kindness and generosity. Your encouragement, on many levels, has given me the ability to persevere through some of the most challenging and difficult times while completing this manuscript. This small book is big in truth. It has given me a voice to express what so many refuse to hear and others decline to admit; THE TRUTH ABOUT SELF!!

My husband and children: Thank you for making my life worth living. I love you to life!

Mom: I'd like to dedicate to you the song, "Mama" by Candi Staton.

Words cannot express how grateful I am for your unfailing love.

Pat Hosley: Thank you for holding me accountable during some of the most challenging seasons in my life.

Mother Lundy: Thank you for teaching me the true meaning of consecration.

My fivefold friends: Denise, Felise, Marcia, Camilla, Karen. Our seasons together will never be forgotten. You're the best!

Carrie Matthews: What can I say? You gave me truth and you never left me. You continued to love me unconditionally. Thank you! God bless your soul, my dear sister/friend. My daughter couldn't have a better Godmother. I love you.

Bishop Clarence and Dorothy Givens; Bishop Mitch and Nancy Way; Pastor Anthony and Margarette Davis; Pastor Dr. Eric and Bloneva Jones: Thank you for answering the call of God. And most of all, thank you for your unconditional love, friendship, mentorship, and leadership. Your direct tutelage has provided divine protection and guardianship over my soul. God has a special place in heaven for people like you. It's people like you who make good leaders great.

Racheal Galvin: Thank you for assisting me in my final stages of completion of this book.

Notes

Notes

Notes

Notes

www.ingramcontent.com/pod-product-compliance
Lightning Source LLC
Chambersburg PA
CBHW071633040426
42452CB00009B/1609